These are the personal references for:

Name

Teresa Rattles

Date of Birth

Nov. 22, 1978

Tree Sign

Reed

Lunar Symbol

White Hound

Lunar Position

Leo

Planetary Ruler

Pluto

Numbers from the Tables of Years				
S	Mn	Mer	Ven	Mars
24	14	26	22	26
Ju	Sat	Ur	Nep	Pl
13	17	--		20

Basic Paragl

137

Conjunctions

196, 230, 0

Aspects

△267, △164, ♦164,
176 △270, △276, ⊾
236, 253, 223
△256

These are the personal references for:

Name

Date of Birth

Tree Sign

Lunar Symbol

Lunar Position

Planetary Ruler

Numbers from the Tables of Years				
S	Mn	Mer	Ven	Mars
Ju	Sat	Ur	Nep	Pl

Basic Paragraph

Conjunctions

Aspects

These are the personal references for:

Name

....

Date of Birth

....

Tree Sign

....

Lunar Symbol

....

Lunar Position

....

Planetary Ruler

....

Numbers from the Tables of Years				
S	Mn	Mer	Ven	Mars
Ju	Sat	Ur	Nep	Pl

Basic Paragraph

....

Conjunctions

....

Aspects

....

These are the personal references for:

Name

Date of Birth

Tree Sign

Lunar Symbol

Lunar Position

Planetary Ruler

Numbers from the Tables of Years				
S	Mn	Mer	Ven	Mars
Ju	Sat	Ur	Nep	Pl

Basic Paragraph

Conjunctions

Aspects

These are the personal references for:

Name

Date of Birth

Tree Sign

Lunar Symbol

Lunar Position

Planetary Ruler

Numbers from the Tables of Years				
S	Mn	Mer	Ven	Mars
Ju	Sat	Ur	Nep	Pl

Basic Paragraph

Conjunctions

Aspects

These are the personal references for:

Name

Date of Birth

Tree Sign

Lunar Symbol

Lunar Position

Planetary Ruler

Numbers from the Tables of Years				
S	Mn	Mer	Ven	Mars
Ju	Sat	Ur	Nep	Pl

Basic Paragraph

Conjunctions

Aspects

These are the personal references for:

Name

Date of Birth

Tree Sign

Lunar Symbol

Lunar Position

Planetary Ruler

Numbers from the Tables of Years				
S	Mn	Mer	Ven	Mars
Ju	Sat	Ur	Nep	Pl

Basic Paragraph

Conjunctions

Aspects

These are the personal references for:

Name

....

Date of Birth

....

Tree Sign

....

Lunar Symbol

....

Lunar Position

....

Planetary Ruler

....

Numbers from the Tables of Years				
S	Mn	Mer	Ven	Mars
Ju	Sat	Ur	Nep	Pl

Basic Paragraph

....

Conjunctions

....

Aspects

....

These are the personal references for:

Name

Date of Birth

Tree Sign

Lunar Symbol

Lunar Position

Planetary Ruler

Numbers from the Tables of Years				
S	Mn	Mer	Ven	Mars
Ju	Sat	Ur	Nep	Pl

Basic Paragraph

Conjunctions

Aspects

These are the personal references for:

Name

Date of Birth

Tree Sign

Lunar Symbol

Lunar Position

Planetary Ruler

Numbers from the Tables of Years				
S	Mn	Mer	Ven	Mars
Ju	Sat	Ur	Nep	Pl

Basic Paragraph

Conjunctions

Aspects

These are the personal references for:

Name

Date of Birth

Tree Sign

Lunar Symbol

Lunar Position

Planetary Ruler

Numbers from the Tables of Years				
S	Mn	Mer	Ven	Mars
Ju	Sat	Ur	Nep	Pl

Basic Paragraph

Conjunctions

Aspects

These are the personal references for:

Name

....

Date of Birth

....

Tree Sign

....

Lunar Symbol

....

Lunar Position

....

Planetary Ruler

....

Numbers from the Tables of Years				
S	Mn	Mer	Ven	Mars
Ju	Sat	Ur	Nep	Pl

Basic Paragraph

....

Conjunctions

....

Aspects

....

These are the personal references for:

Name

....

Date of Birth

....

Tree Sign

....

Lunar Symbol

....

Lunar Position

....

Planetary Ruler

....

Numbers from the Tables of Years				
S	Mn	Mer	Ven	Mars
Ju	Sat	Ur	Nep	Pl

Basic Paragraph

....

Conjunctions

....

Aspects

....

These are the personal references for:

Name

....

Date of Birth

....

Tree Sign

....

Lunar Symbol

....

Lunar Position

....

Planetary Ruler

....

Numbers from the Tables of Years				
S	Mn	Mer	Ven	Mars
Ju	Sat	Ur	Nep	Pl

Basic Paragraph

....

Conjunctions

....

Aspects

....

These are the personal references for:

Name
....

Date of Birth
....

Tree Sign   .
....

Lunar Symbol
....

Lunar Position
....

Planetary Ruler
....

Numbers from the Tables of Years				
S	Mn	Mer	Ven	Mars
Ju	Sat	Ur	Nep	Pl

Basic Paragraph
....

Conjunctions
....

Aspects
....

These are the personal references for:

Name

Date of Birth

Tree Sign

Lunar Symbol

Lunar Position

Planetary Ruler

Numbers from the Tables of Years				
S	Mn	Mer	Ven	Mars
Ju	Sat	Ur	Nep	Pl

Basic Paragraph

Conjunctions

Aspects

These are the personal references for:

Name

Date of Birth

Tree Sign

Lunar Symbol

Lunar Position

Planetary Ruler

Numbers from the Tables of Years				
S	Mn	Mer	Ven	Mars
Ju	Sat	Ur	Nep	Pl

Basic Paragraph

Conjunctions

Aspects

These are the personal references for:

Name

Date of Birth

Tree Sign

Lunar Symbol

Lunar Position

Planetary Ruler

Numbers from the Tables of Years				
S	Mn	Mer	Ven	Mars
Ju	Sat	Ur	Nep	Pl

Basic Paragraph

Conjunctions

Aspects

These are the personal references for:

Name

Date of Birth

Tree Sign

Lunar Symbol

Lunar Position

Planetary Ruler

Numbers from the Tables of Years				
S	Mn	Mer	Ven	Mars
Ju	Sat	Ur	Nep	Pl

Basic Paragraph

Conjunctions

Aspects

These are the personal references for:

Name

Date of Birth

Tree Sign

Lunar Symbol

Lunar Position

Planetary Ruler

Numbers from the Tables of Years				
S	Mn	Mer	Ven	Mars
Ju	Sat	Ur	Nep	Pl

Basic Paragraph

Conjunctions

Aspects

These are the personal references for:

Name

Date of Birth

Tree Sign

Lunar Symbol

Lunar Position

Planetary Ruler

Numbers from the Tables of Years				
S	Mn	Mer	Ven	Mars
Ju	Sat	Ur	Nep	Pl

Basic Paragraph

Conjunctions

Aspects

These are the personal references for:

Name

Date of Birth

Tree Sign

Lunar Symbol

Lunar Position

Planetary Ruler

Numbers from the Tables of Years				
S	Mn	Mer	Ven	Mars
Ju	Sat	Ur	Nep	Pl

Basic Paragraph

Conjunctions

Aspects

These are the personal references for:

Name

....

Date of Birth

....

Tree Sign

....

Lunar Symbol

....

Lunar Position

....

Planetary Ruler

....

Numbers from the Tables of Years				
S	Mn	Mer	Ven	Mars
Ju	Sat	Ur	Nep	Pl

Basic Paragraph

....

Conjunctions

....

Aspects

....

These are the personal references for:

Name

Date of Birth

Tree Sign

Lunar Symbol

Lunar Position

Planetary Ruler

Numbers from the Tables of Years				
S	Mn	Mer	Ven	Mars
Ju	Sat	Ur	Nep	Pl

Basic Paragraph

Conjunctions

Aspects

These are the personal references for:

Name

Date of Birth

Tree Sign

Lunar Symbol

Lunar Position

Planetary Ruler

Numbers from the Tables of Years				
S	Mn	Mer	Ven	Mars
Ju	Sat	Ur	Nep	Pl

Basic Paragraph

Conjunctions

Aspects

These are the personal references for:

Name

Date of Birth

Tree Sign

Lunar Symbol

Lunar Position

Planetary Ruler

Numbers from the Tables of Years				
S	Mn	Mer	Ven	Mars
Ju	Sat	Ur	Nep	Pl

Basic Paragraph

Conjunctions

Aspects

These are the personal references for:

Name

Date of Birth

Tree Sign

Lunar Symbol

Lunar Position

Planetary Ruler

Numbers from the Tables of Years				
S	Mn	Mer	Ven	Mars
Ju	Sat	Ur	Nep	Pl

Basic Paragraph

Conjunctions

Aspects

These are the personal references for:

Name

Date of Birth

Tree Sign

Lunar Symbol

Lunar Position

Planetary Ruler

Numbers from the Tables of Years				
S	Mn	Mer	Ven	Mars
Ju	Sat	Ur	Nep	Pl

Basic Paragraph

Conjunctions

Aspects

These are the personal references for:

Name

Date of Birth

Tree Sign

Lunar Symbol

Lunar Position

Planetary Ruler

Numbers from the Tables of Years				
S	Mn	Mer	Ven	Mars
Ju	Sat	Ur	Nep	Pl

Basic Paragraph

Conjunctions

Aspects

These are the personal references for:

Name

Date of Birth

Tree Sign

Lunar Symbol

Lunar Position

Planetary Ruler

Numbers from the Tables of Years				
S	Mn	Mer	Ven	Mars
Ju	Sat	Ur	Nep	Pl

Basic Paragraph

Conjunctions

Aspects

These are the personal references for:

Name

....

Date of Birth

....

Tree Sign

....

Lunar Symbol

....

Lunar Position

....

Planetary Ruler

....

Numbers from the Tables of Years				
S	Mn	Mer	Ven	Mars
Ju	Sat	Ur	Nep	Pl

Basic Paragraph

....

Conjunctions

....

Aspects

....

These are the personal references for:

Name

Date of Birth

Tree Sign

Lunar Symbol

Lunar Position

Planetary Ruler

Numbers from the Tables of Years				
S	Mn	Mer	Ven	Mars
Ju	Sat	Ur	Nep	Pl

Basic Paragraph

Conjunctions

Aspects

These are the personal references for:

Name

....

Date of Birth

....

Tree Sign

....

Lunar Symbol

....

Lunar Position

....

Planetary Ruler

....

Numbers from the Tables of Years				
S	Mn	Mer	Ven	Mars
Ju	Sat	Ur	Nep	Pl

Basic Paragraph

....

Conjunctions

....

Aspects

....

These are the personal references for:

Name

Date of Birth

Tree Sign

Lunar Symbol

Lunar Position

Planetary Ruler

Numbers from the Tables of Years				
S	Mn	Mer	Ven	Mars
Ju	Sat	Ur	Nep	Pl

Basic Paragraph

Conjunctions

Aspects

These are the personal references for:

Name

Date of Birth

Tree Sign

Lunar Symbol

Lunar Position

Planetary Ruler

Numbers from the Tables of Years				
S	Mn	Mer	Ven	Mars
Ju	Sat	Ur	Nep	Pl

Basic Paragraph

Conjunctions

Aspects

These are the personal references for:

Name

Date of Birth

Tree Sign

Lunar Symbol

Lunar Position

Planetary Ruler

Numbers from the Tables of Years				
S	Mn	Mer	Ven	Mars
Ju	Sat	Ur	Nep	Pl

Basic Paragraph

Conjunctions

Aspects

These are the personal references for:

Name

Date of Birth

Tree Sign

Lunar Symbol

Lunar Position

Planetary Ruler

Numbers from the Tables of Years				
S	Mn	Mer	Ven	Mars
Ju	Sat	Ur	Nep	Pl

Basic Paragraph

Conjunctions

Aspects

These are the personal references for:

Name

Date of Birth

Tree Sign

Lunar Symbol

Lunar Position

Planetary Ruler

Numbers from the Tables of Years				
S	Mn	Mer	Ven	Mars
Ju	Sat	Ur	Nep	Pl

Basic Paragraph

Conjunctions

Aspects

These are the personal references for:

Name

Date of Birth

Tree Sign

Lunar Symbol

Lunar Position

Planetary Ruler

Numbers from the Tables of Years				
S	Mn	Mer	Ven	Mars
Ju	Sat	Ur	Nep	Pl

Basic Paragraph

Conjunctions

Aspects

These are the personal references for:

Name

Date of Birth

Tree Sign

Lunar Symbol

Lunar Position

Planetary Ruler

Numbers from the Tables of Years				
S	Mn	Mer	Ven	Mars
Ju	Sat	Ur	Nep	Pl

Basic Paragraph

Conjunctions

Aspects

These are the personal references for:

Name

....

Date of Birth

....

Tree Sign

....

Lunar Symbol

....

Lunar Position

....

Planetary Ruler

....

Numbers from the Tables of Years				
S	Mn	Mer	Ven	Mars
Ju	Sat	Ur	Nep	Pl

Basic Paragraph

....

Conjunctions

....

Aspects

....

These are the personal references for:

Name

....

Date of Birth

....

Tree Sign

....

Lunar Symbol

....

Lunar Position

....

Planetary Ruler

....

Numbers from the Tables of Years				
S	Mn	Mer	Ven	Mars
Ju	Sat	Ur	Nep	Pl

Basic Paragraph

....

Conjunctions

....

Aspects

....

These are the personal references for:

Name

...

Date of Birth

...

Tree Sign

...

Lunar Symbol

...

Lunar Position

...

Planetary Ruler

...

Numbers from the Tables of Years				
S	Mn	Mer	Ven	Mars
Ju	Sat	Ur·	Nep	Pl

Basic Paragraph

...

Conjunctions

...

Aspects

...

These are the personal references for:

Name

Date of Birth

Tree Sign

Lunar Symbol

Lunar Position

Planetary Ruler

Numbers from the Tables of Years				
S	Mn	Mer	Ven	Mars
Ju	Sat	Ur	Nep	Pl

Basic Paragraph

Conjunctions

Aspects

These are the personal references for:

Name

Date of Birth

Tree Sign

Lunar Symbol

Lunar Position

Planetary Ruler

Numbers from the Tables of Years				
S	Mn	Mer	Ven	Mars
Ju	Sat	Ur	Nep	Pl

Basic Paragraph

Conjunctions

Aspects

These are the personal references for:

Name

Date of Birth

Tree Sign

Lunar Symbol

Lunar Position

Planetary Ruler

Numbers from the Tables of Years				
S	Mn	Mer	Ven	Mars
Ju	Sat	Ur	Nep	Pl

Basic Paragraph

Conjunctions

Aspects

These are the personal references for:

Name
....

Date of Birth
....

Tree Sign
....

Lunar Symbol
....

Lunar Position
....

Planetary Ruler
....

Numbers from the Tables of Years				
S	Mn	Mer	Ven	Mars
Ju	Sat	Ur	Nep	Pl

Basic Paragraph
....

Conjunctions
....

Aspects
....

These are the personal references for:

Name

Date of Birth

Tree Sign

Lunar Symbol

Lunar Position

Planetary Ruler

Numbers from the Tables of Years				
S	Mn	Mer	Ven	Mars
Ju	Sat	Ur	Nep	Pl

Basic Paragraph

Conjunctions

Aspects

These are the personal references for:

Name

Date of Birth

Tree Sign

Lunar Symbol

Lunar Position

Planetary Ruler

Numbers from the Tables of Years				
S	Mn	Mer	Ven	Mars
Ju	Sat	Ur	Nep	Pl

Basic Paragraph

Conjunctions

Aspects

These are the personal references for:

Name
....

Date of Birth
....

Tree Sign
....

Lunar Symbol
....

Lunar Position
....

Planetary Ruler
....

Numbers from the Tables of Years				
S	Mn	Mer	Ven	Mars
Ju	Sat	Ur	Nep	Pl

Basic Paragraph
....

Conjunctions
....

Aspects
....

These are the personal references for:

Name

Date of Birth

Tree Sign

Lunar Symbol

Lunar Position

Planetary Ruler

Numbers from the Tables of Years				
S	Mn	Mer	Ven	Mars
Ju	Sat	Ur	Nep	Pl

Basic Paragraph

Conjunctions

Aspects

These are the personal references for:

Name

Date of Birth

Tree Sign

Lunar Symbol

Lunar Position

Planetary Ruler

Numbers from the Tables of Years				
S	Mn	Mer	Ven	Mars
Ju	Sat	Ur	Nep	Pl

Basic Paragraph

Conjunctions

Aspects

These are the personal references for:

Name

....

Date of Birth

....

Tree Sign

....

Lunar Symbol

....

Lunar Position

....

Planetary Ruler

....

Numbers from the Tables of Years				
S	Mn	Mer	Ven	Mars
Ju	Sat	Ur	Nep	Pl

Basic Paragraph

....

Conjunctions

....

Aspects

....

These are the personal references for:

Name

Date of Birth

Tree Sign

Lunar Symbol

Lunar Position

Planetary Ruler

Numbers from the Tables of Years				
S	Mn	Mer	Ven	Mars
Ju	Sat	Ur	Nep	Pl

Basic Paragraph

Conjunctions

Aspects

These are the personal references for:

Name
....

Date of Birth
....

Tree Sign
....

Lunar Symbol
....

Lunar Position
....

Planetary Ruler
....

Numbers from the Tables of Years				
S	Mn	Mer	Ven	Mars
Ju	Sat	Ur	Nep	Pl

Basic Paragraph
....

Conjunctions
....

Aspects
....

These are the personal references for:

Name
....

Date of Birth
....

Tree Sign
....

Lunar Symbol
....

Lunar Position
....

Planetary Ruler
....

Numbers from the Tables of Years				
S	Mn	Mer	Ven	Mars
Ju	Sat	Ur	Nep	Pl

Basic Paragraph
....

Conjunctions
....

Aspects
....

These are the personal references for:

Name

Date of Birth

Tree Sign

Lunar Symbol

Lunar Position

Planetary Ruler

Numbers from the Tables of Years				
S	Mn	Mer	Ven	Mars
Ju	Sat	Ur	Nep	Pl

Basic Paragraph

Conjunctions

Aspects

These are the personal references for:

Name

....

Date of Birth

....

Tree Sign

....

Lunar Symbol

....

Lunar Position

....

Planetary Ruler

....

Numbers from the Tables of Years				
S	Mn	Mer	Ven	Mars
Ju	Sat	Ur	Nep	Pl

Basic Paragraph

....

Conjunctions

....

Aspects

....

These are the personal references for:

Name

....

Date of Birth

....

Tree Sign

....

Lunar Symbol

....

Lunar Position

....

Planetary Ruler

....

Numbers from the Tables of Years				
S	Mn	Mer	Ven	Mars
Ju	Sat	Ur	Nep	pl

Basic Paragraph

....

Conjunctions

....

Aspects

....

These are the personal references for:

Name

....

Date of Birth

....

Tree Sign

....

Lunar Symbol

....

Lunar Position

....

Planetary Ruler

....

Numbers from the Tables of Years				
S	Mn	Mer	Ven	Mars
Ju	Sat	Ur	Nep	Pl

Basic Paragraph

....

Conjunctions

....

Aspects

....

These are the personal references for:

Name

Date of Birth

Tree Sign

Lunar Symbol

Lunar Position

Planetary Ruler

Numbers from the Tables of Years				
S	Mn	Mer	Ven	Mars
Ju	Sat	Ur	Nep	Pl

Basic Paragraph

Conjunctions

Aspects